Yasmeen Lari, Green Architect

The True Story of Pakistan's First Woman Architect

Written by **Marzieh Abbas**   Illustrated by **Hoda Hadadi**

CLARION BOOKS
An Imprint of HarperCollins*Publishers*

Even when she was little, Yasmeen Lari was a great listener.

And that made her a great learner, too.

When Yasmeen was six, her country split in two—India and Pakistan.

Yasmeen's parents welcomed hot, hungry, homeless refugees.

Her baba oversaw the construction of shelters.

Her mama cooked fancy desserts to raise funds. As the seasons passed,

Yasmeen grew.

She observed.

She helped.

She admired.

She celebrated.

Her mama and baba encouraged her and her sister to achieve great things, just like her brother.

Yasmeen continued to listen and learn. Two degrees, a marriage, and eight years later, Yasmeen became Pakistan's first woman architect.

She set up her practice in Karachi, the buzzing city by the sea.

Rich, powerful clients flocked to Yasmeen's office.
They were fickle and tough.
But Yasmeen was up for the challenge.

She envisioned.

She measured.

She drew.

She instructed.

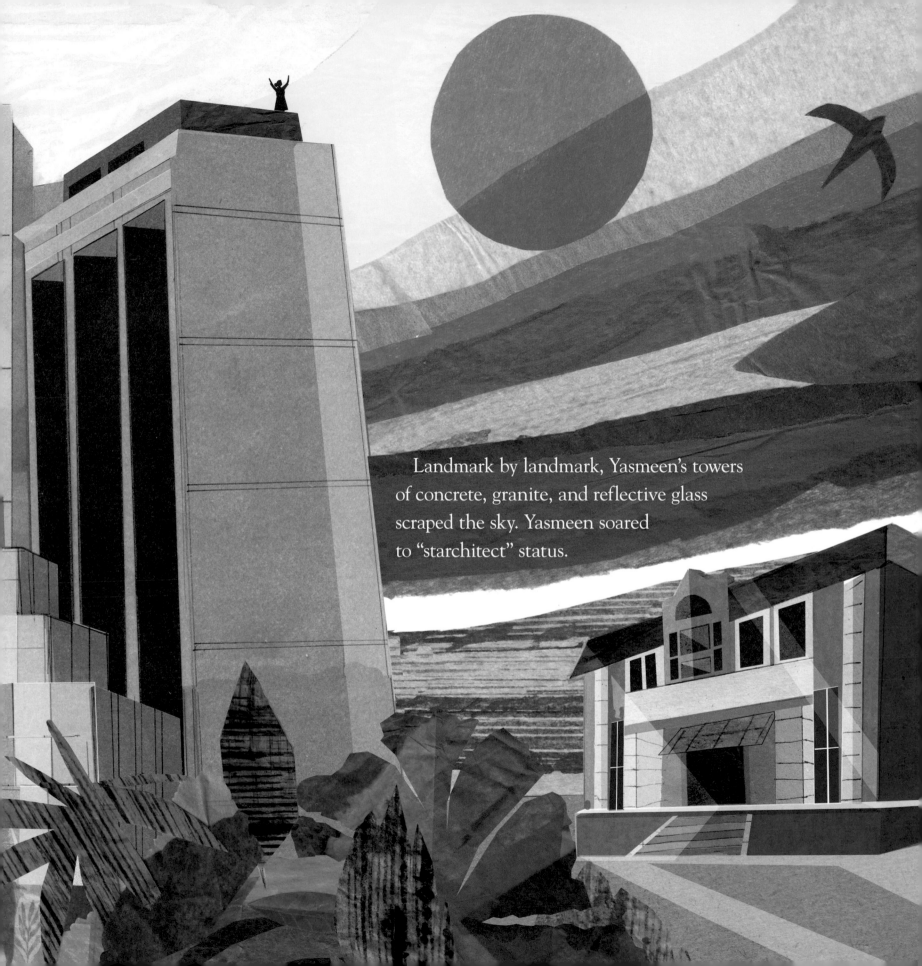

Landmark by landmark, Yasmeen's towers
of concrete, granite, and reflective glass
scraped the sky. Yasmeen soared
to "starchitect" status.

In between construction projects, Yasmeen explored old towns and villages with her husband, Suhail, a historian and photographer.

She toured.

She studied.

lime

soil

Lime = 30%
Mud = 30%
water = 40%

She noted.

She appreciated.

Her heart swelled with pride as she
dug deeper into her roots.

But soon, Yasmeen
noticed a disturbing trend.

Urban developers tore down historic buildings to make way for malls and offices. Modern building materials—concrete and graphite—were shrouding urban centers in shades of gray.

Cities around Pakistan were losing their distinct character. Pakistanis were outraged. Historic buildings had to be protected.

At the time, most believed only men could raise their voices for a cause. Yasmeen thought their mindsets were more ancient than the buildings she was fighting to conserve.

She listened to their arguments.

She raised her voice against them.

She challenged their outlook.

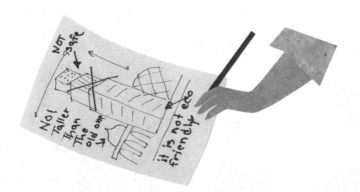

She dug deep for a creative solution.

Week after week . . .

Yasmeen pulled her community together to conserve historic sites in cities across Pakistan. An army of students, professors, journalists, and lovers of art and history came out of their homes to protect their history in a cultural street fest.

Revive
The
Spirit
of
Karachi

Treat Karachi like home

Finally, a breakthrough!
The government took notice.

Government Of Pakistan Heritage

SINDH cultural Heritage

(Preservation) Act
Enacted

Heritage
PAKISTAN

The historic buildings were declared heritage sites.
No one could demolish them.

Next, Yasmeen
worked towards
restoration.

Scratch.
Scrape.
Scrub.

Yasmeen and her helpers gently chipped away grime with grit.
Word soon spread about Yasmeen's conservation work.

She was invited
to lead an ancient fort
conservation project.
By day, she instructed foreign
engineers and architects on her
team. By night, the keys to the
fort and all its secret chambers
jingled in Yasmeen's hands—an open
invitation to travel through history.

She roamed the fort's
archways, admired murals,
ran her hands over elaborate
tilework, and glided through
pearl-white marble corridors. The
vernacular architecture and mud-lime
plastering techniques amazed Yasmeen.
Peace and grandeur enveloped her in the
folds of history.
But peace was suddenly shattered . . .

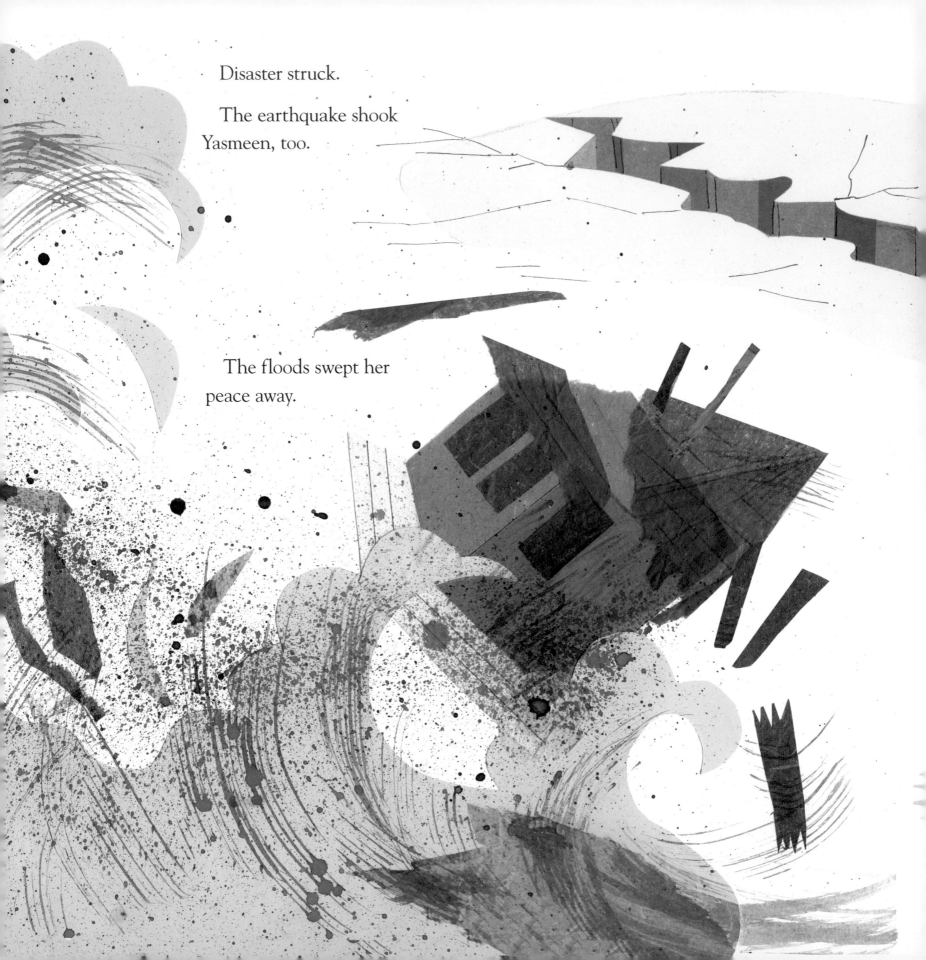

Disaster struck.

The earthquake shook
Yasmeen, too.

The floods swept her
peace away.

Yasmeen witnessed:

Mounds of rubble.

Bent metal.

Fierce floods.

Building for rehabilitation
was unlike any work she had
ever done.

Yasmeen listened:

To the woes of the villagers.

To the pleas of the planet.

Yasmeen listed the challenges:

No shelter.

No drainage.

Poverty.

Ticking clocks.

Extreme temperatures.

Would Yasmeen rise to the challenge?

Yasmeen learned about local building traditions.

Villagers in the earthquake-prone areas used wooden cross-braced frames to strengthen walls.

Those in the flood-prone areas used readily available riverside mud to build their huts.

Yasmeen wanted to fuse their tried-and-tested techniques with her knowledge of design.

Yasmeen pondered over tough questions:
Are mud huts strong enough?
After all these years, how are ancient heritage buildings still standing?
Can low-cost structures be built?
Can we build for all villagers to be safe?
Is it possible to build in an eco-friendly way?

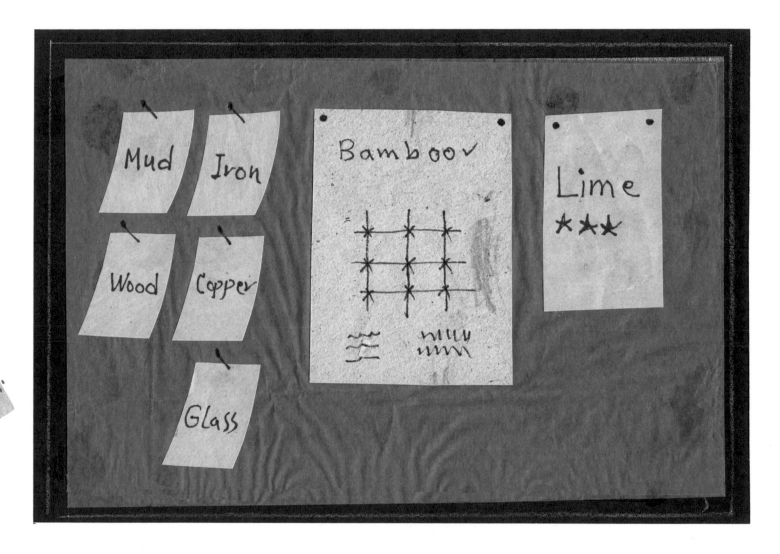

Yasmeen dug into her notes.
She recalled the vernacular architecture from her travels around Pakistan.
She remembered that lime was added to mud for extra durability.

Yasmeen set herself a challenge:

Zero waste.   Low cost.   Zero carbon.

Yasmeen narrowed down her building material options:

No to fuel-intensive, carbon-emitting materials.

No to concrete.   No to metal.   No to graphite.

No to glass.   No to wood.

Yes to renewable, eco-friendly, natural materials.

Yes to bamboo.   Yes to mud.   Yes to lime.

Yasmeen designed and sketched.
For the earthquake-prone areas, she suggested bamboo crisscrossing lattice sandwiching mud-lime brick walls from ground to ceiling.

For the flood-prone areas, she proposed hexagonal structures of mud-lime brick walls to be positioned on bamboo stilts, eight feet high.

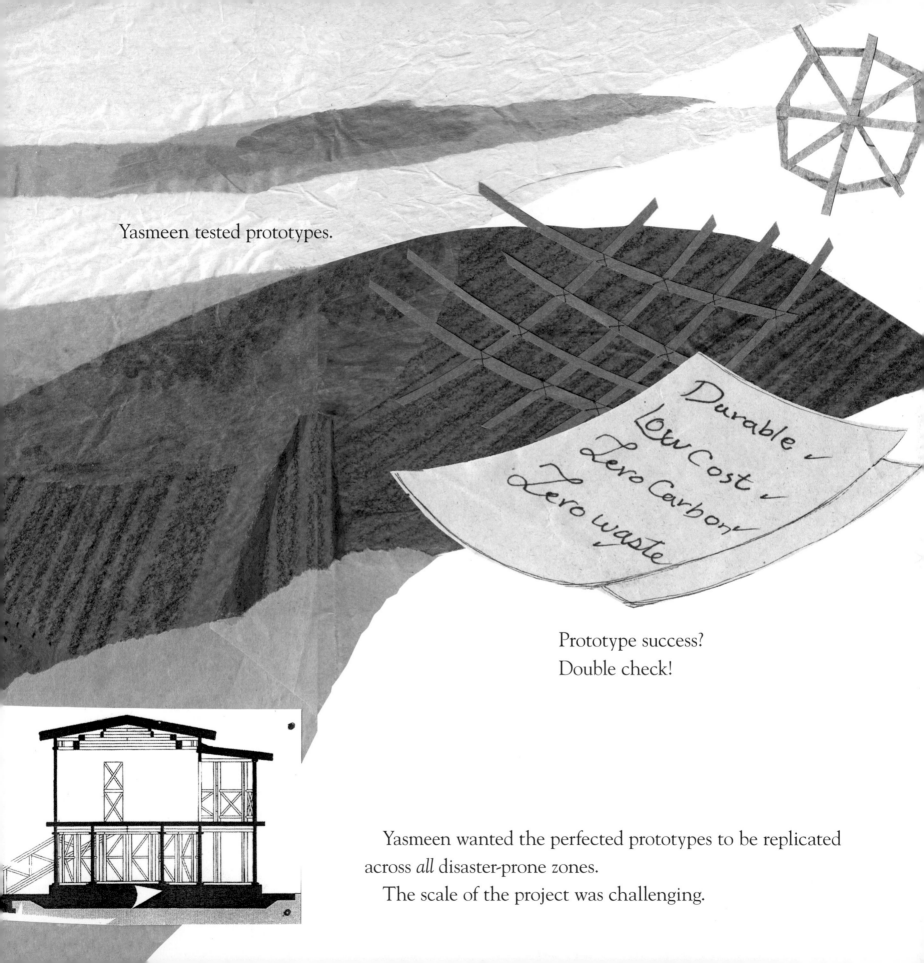

Yasmeen tested prototypes.

Durable ✓
Low Cost ✓
Zero Carbon ✓
Zero waste ✓

Prototype success?
Double check!

Yasmeen wanted the perfected prototypes to be replicated across *all* disaster-prone zones.

The scale of the project was challenging.

Yasmeen had an idea—*cocreation*!
She would train the poverty-stricken
villagers to build their own houses.

Then they would travel to other
villages and train more villagers.

Yasmeen rebuilt lives. The
villagers were:

Trained.

Equipped.

Determined.

The villagers
were ready to build!

Mud-lime bricks.

Bamboo sticks.

Mud splat.

Roof thatch.

In a few years, Yasmeen's "barefoot architecture" blueprint had been used to build 40,000 disaster-resistant homes. Awards, titles, and accolades shone the spotlight on Yasmeen.

She shone the spotlight on Pakistan's heritage: culture, traditions, and history.

Yasmeen had tackled every challenge that came her way.
She'd listened to the pleas of the planet and the woes of the villagers.

Now, the world listens
to Yasmeen.

More about Yasmeen Lari

"Everywhere I've been I try to see that I design something using traditional materials, but doing (so) in a manner that improves the lives of people."
—Yasmeen Lari

Born in 1941, Yasmeen grew up in a privileged, elite household in the Punjab province. Her father held a government position in pre-partitioned India. After partition, he was in charge of developing acres upon acres of land of the newly formed state, Pakistan. Yasmeen grew up hearing her father saying "this country needs architects." Since there weren't any local architects at the time, Yasmeen wished to fulfill her father's dreams. When she got the chance to study abroad, Yasmeen graduated from the now Oxford Brookes University.

Upon her return to Pakistan, Yasmeen set up her private practice and built grand structures and sprawling housing schemes. When Yasmeen explored the ancient towns of Pakistan with her husband, Suhail Zaheer Lari, a prominent historian and photographer, she appreciated the culture, traditions, and vernacular architecture of the Indus Valley Civilization. Together they founded the Heritage Foundation of Pakistan (HFP) aiming to "document and conserve the traditional and historic built environment of Pakistan." Their efforts were soon recognized by the United Nations Educational, Scientific and Cultural Organization (UNESCO).

In 2005, when an earthquake struck northern Pakistan, Yasmeen joined throngs of volunteers and humanitarian agencies to do whatever she could to help. She wanted the villagers to feel involved and take pride in the construction process and outcome. Yasmeen taught them the basic principles for creating stable structures while respecting their knowledge of the use of accessible, locally sourced material and techniques that had been passed down for generations. The villagers used her open-source blueprints and customized the structures to suit their own needs.

Between 2005 and 2015, several more disasters hit Pakistan. It was also increasingly clear that climate change was a growing issue. Yasmeen knew it was time to use more eco-friendly materials. The wood that the locals used for construction in the north was adding to deforestation and subsequent flooding further down south.

Along with housing solutions, Yasmeen worked with international experts to design eco-toilets, raised hand pumps, and earthen stoves—*chulahs*—for the flood- and earthquake-prone communities. Along with helping to rebuild houses, Yasmeen gave special attention to women's upliftment and organized workshops for training the locals in ceramic *Kashi* crafts. The communities she worked in were so poor, they mostly roamed barefoot. This led Yasmeen to coin the term BaSA, "Barefoot Social Architecture." This was a holistic approach to rights-based development.

Even in her eighties, Yasmeen continues to encourage the use of zero-carbon materials amongst displaced populations of Pakistan and shares her open-source approach worldwide through the Heritage Foundation of Pakistan.

Author's Note

Growing up in Karachi, Pakistan, I crossed a famous landmark, the Finance and Trade Centre, on my way to school every day. Little did I know that the building was designed by Pakistan's first woman architect, Yasmeen Lari.

Over the course of the extensive primary and secondary research I did for this biography, including several interviews with Yasmeen, I learned about her journey firsthand—from her protected, privileged childhood as the daughter of a high-level civil servant of British India to becoming an accomplished star architect: "starchitect." However, the most meaningful part of her journey began after she retired from her private practice and evolved into a humanitarian "barefoot architect." In the interviews I personally conducted with Yasmeen, and in the many that I viewed, Yasmeen was most passionate about her work for underserved communities.

Glossary

"Barefoot Architecture"—the practice of designing and constructing for underserved communities that cannot afford shoes

Conservation—preservation and repair of archaeological, historical, and cultural sites and artefacts

Heritage—denoting or relating to things of special architectural, historical, or natural value that are preserved for the nation

Restoration—the process of returning a building or work of art to its original condition

Rehabilitation—the action of restoring someone who has been displaced and disadvantaged to a better condition

"Starchitect"—a famous or high-profile architect

Vernacular architecture—a type of architecture used to build domestic housing that reflects local traditions and cultural practices. The structures built are functional and use easily available, indigenous material.

Zero carbon—a process that produces no carbon emissions and hence is eco-friendly

Yasmeen Lari's Time Line

Architect Yasmeen Lari overseeing the construction of a zero-carbon, low-cost structure

Yasmeen demonstrating conservation techniques to student volunteers in Karachi, Pakistan

Yasmeen stands against a mud-lime brick wall at the Makli Necropolis, Thatta, one of the largest funeral sites in the world, dating back to the fourteenth century.

A hut designed by Yasmeen built on stilts in the flood-prone villages of the southern province of Sindh, Pakistan

Cross-braced earthquake resistant bamboo structures designed by Yasmeen in Swat, northern Pakistan

1941
Born in
Dera Ghazi Khan

1947
Partition of Indian
subcontinent into India
and Pakistan

1956
Left Pakistan to
study in London
and Oxford

1963
Graduated from
Oxford School
of Architecture

1964
Established architectural
practice: Lari Associates,
Architects and
Urban Designers

1969
Elected to Royal
Institute of British
Architects

1989
Designed and built
Karachi's Finance
and Trade Centre

1991
Designed and built the
Pakistan State Oil
House in Karachi

2000
Closed Lari Associates

Coauthored city guides
and books on heritage

2003
Advisor to UNESCO
on Lahore Fort
conservation project

2005
Earthquake in
northern Pakistan

Yasmeen sharing her BaSA (Barefoot Social Architecture) philosophy with the world in a Zoom meeting conducted during the pandemic

Yasmeen at the women's center during a training session for the women villagers in Sindh. The center is built on stilts using traditional materials and techniques to withstand the floods in the region.

1978
Designed and built the Anguri Bagh Housing Project

1981
Established Heritage Foundation of Pakistan as a Lari family trust and developed source material on Pakistan's cultural heritage, shifting focus from new construction to preservation

1981
Designed and built Taj Mahal Hotel in Karachi

1982
Designed and built the Lines Area Resettlement Project

1987
Initiated Heritage Foundation of Pakistan's National Register of Historic Places by cataloguing Karachi's urban assets in order to provide them with legal protection

2007
Started working in bamboo

2009
Played an important role in rehabilitation for villagers displaced by Taliban militia

2010
Severe floods in southern Pakistan

2018
Founding chairwoman of the International Network for Traditional Building, Architecture and Urbanism

2020
In the process of designing floating house structures for areas affected by severe flooding

Selected Sources

Abbas, Marzieh. "Interview with Yasmeen Lari." January 7, 2021.

AlJazeeraEnglish. "Rebel Architecture - A Traditional Future." YouTube, August 26, 2014. youtube.com/watch?v=5yvAFis1FB0&t=1s.

Architectural Review. "Yasmeen Lari: 'Architects Can No Longer Only Serve the 1%.'" YouTube. YouTube, March 23, 2020. youtube.com/watch?v=HqxOn4tdvKQ.

Haneef, Rabia. "'Architects Have to Be Really Sensitive about Their Own Traditions' Says Yasmeen Lari." World Architecture Community, October 15, 2020. worldarchitecture.org/article-links/eghgv/-architects-have-to-be-really-sensitive-about-their-own-traditions-says-yasmeen-lari.html.

Ramzi, Shanaz. "Retrospective: Yasmeen Lari." *Architectural Review*, September 9, 2019. architectural-review.com/buildings/retrospective-yasmeen-lari.

Sangster, Celeste. "Celebrating Extraordinary Women: Yasmeen Lari." World Habitat, March 8, 2019. world-habitat.org/news/our-blog/celebrating-extraordinary-women-yasmeen-lari/.

Thomas, Helen. "Yasmeen Lari: Drawn Closer." Drawing Matter, April 7, 2020. drawingmatter.org/yasmeen-lari-drawn-closer/.

Wainwright, Oliver. "The Barefoot Architect: 'I Was a Starchitect for 36 Years. Now I'm Atoning.'" *Guardian*, April 1, 2020. theguardian.com/artanddesign/2020/apr/01/yasmeen-lari-pakistan-architect-first-female-jane-drew.

To Yasmeen (Lari) Aunty, who during the course of research for this book taught me
so much about life; perseverance, humility, and grace. May you continue to inspire
children all around the globe to let their creativity soar higher than the tallest
skyscrapers and to speak up and take a stand for our planet and humanity.
—M. A.

To the rough and beautiful hands of my mother.
—H. H.

Clarion Books is an imprint of HarperCollins Publishers.

Yasmeen Lari, Green Architect
Text copyright © 2024 by Marzieh Abbas
Illustrations copyright © 2024 by Hoda Hadadi
Library of Congress Control Number: 2023948816
ISBN 978-0-06-328515-6

The artist used paper collage to create the illustrations for this book.
Typography by Rachel Zegar
24 25 26 27 28 RTLO 10 9 8 7 6 5 4 3 2 1

First Edition